Carousel

Poems and Pictures

Carousel

Poems and Pictures

Merry Christmas
+Happy New Year
to Linda Rogers
+the lutanist of Fleas

~~George Whipple~~

George Whipple

Ekstasis Editions

Canadian Cataloguing in Publication Data

Whipple, George
Carousel.

Poems
ISBN 1-896860-67-2

I. Title.
Ps8595.H39C37   1999   C811'.54   C99-911308-9
PR9199.3.W428C37   1999

Acknowledgements:
Some of these poems first appeared in the following magazines (often in different form): *Candelabrum* (UK), *Green's Magazine*, *Museletter*, *Tidepool*, *Poet's Market* (US). This is the first appearance of the drawings.

Thanks to Farida Ismail, Metro Duplicating, Vancouver, for computer processing.

Published in 1999 by:
Ekstasis Editions Canada Ltd.
Box 8474, Main Postal Outlet
Victoria, B.C. V8W 3S1

THE CANADA COUNCIL | LE CONSEIL DES ARTS
FOR THE ARTS | DU CANADA
SINCE 1957 | DEPUIS 1957

Carousel: Poems and Drawings has been published with the assistance of a grant from the Canada Council and the Cultural Services Branch of British Columbia.

to
The Paraclete
with many thanks
and to
Ralph Cunningham
as always

THE POEMS

Carousel

Poems and Pictures

BODHISATTVA

Nothing is more important than she is:
neither the Four Noble Truths
nor the Eightfold Path to Nirvana,
neither the Way to Wisdom
nor the absence of all desire.

Confronting a huge impassive Buddha
carved from stone and brooding on Emptiness,
a woman stands with her newborn in her arms
— until the granite features seem to break
into a smile of pure Enlightenment.

And so I praise all mothers in that mother
as the whole ocean is in each drop of water.

NEWBORN

POEM POEM

Paper, pencil, stealth,
    wearing sackcloth or motley,
        what else does one need
to rehabilitate the poem,
decriminalize the senses?

Art is everywhere:
    glass tulips in store windows,
        the riposte of a drum
repeating the invaginate slow
heartbeat in the womb;

a predestined rhyme;
    a way for song to flower
        in a cello; for faith
to hold a dancer in mid-air,
all disbelief suspended.

An antic moth
    re-enacts my childhood
        escaping from the closet
of mere time to frolic
in the vineyard of Forever

where voices sing the fierce
    lost language of the soul
        — sole pleasure of my youth,
and only hope, however frail,
of redeeming my last years.

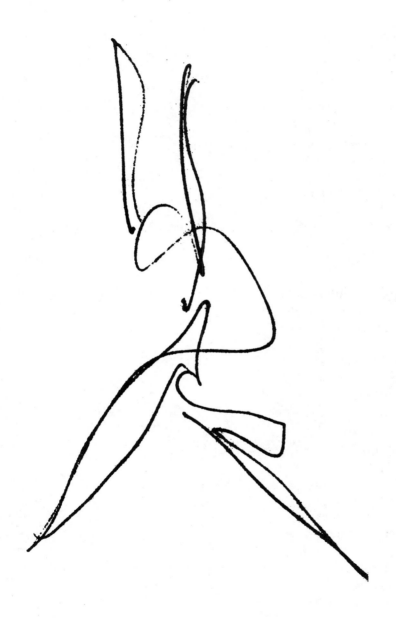

LOOSE CHANGE

Words
are always
a little hungry.

Nothing
pleases them
more than finding

themselves in a poem
where they are fed
by their own singing

— contemporary still
though caged
a thousand

years ago. Although
jazz musicians know
what they know

only by playing,
poets have to wait
for the right

word to come
— as mystics see
the light

only by looking
into the darkness
where it shines

like loose
change beneath the
cushions of a sofa.

PEEWEE   RUSSELL (J)

MUSIC

Fingers float
    over strings; a dance
of body language, hands
and arms moving in unison,
    heads bobbing up and down
as in a trance.

The longer one listens
    the shorter the distance
seems between death and birth,
we are part of all that is and never was
as clouds that pass from one life
    to another in a breath.

Lunar blue
    the low-pitched oboe breathes,
illuminates landscapes of sorrow,
almost explains the death of children;
    on the outskirts of hearing
      a door is opened to knowledge
beyond all other knowing.

All things disappear in time,
    yet in the amber of eternity are kept
      as the saffron light of summer
    in the eerie timbre of a clarinet,
darkness in the shadow of violas.

WEDNESDAY MORNING BLUES

Today is Wednesday
    and the world is round.
When I asked for steak
    you gave me ground.

I remember your eyes,
    your smile, your kisses,
your musical voice
    turned suddenly vicious.

Why did you run away?
    From jealousy or spite?
Why did you run away
    in the dead of the night?

When we kissed, your tongue
    went in and out like a lizard's,
but when you told me lies
    it cut like scissors.

Today is Wednesday
    and the world is round.
When I needed love
    you weren't around,
            you weren't around.

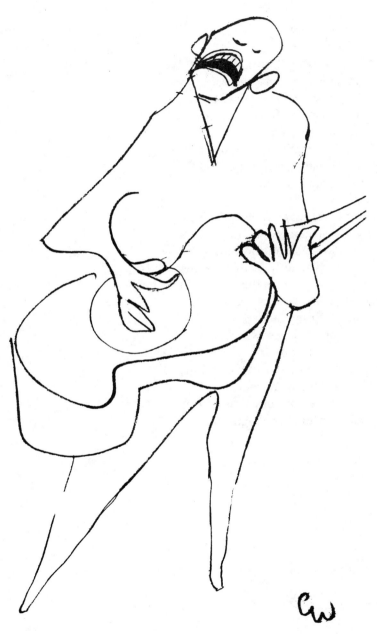

THE CREATIVE INSTANT

As just the right
    colours to a painter
        flock by intuition
    to sing upon his canvas,
and as poems fill the whiteness
    between words with music;
        as the calypso singer
            vibrates with his drumming
        always a few beats ahead
    of where his voice is
making something out of nothing,
yet more intimate than breathing;
    or as skaters leave a kiss
        incised on iridescent ice
            already melting as they soar
                into the future of another
figuration — twisting legs and torsos
    in a twirling saltarello. . .so all
        artists know where they are
            not by where they've been
but only in the instant of creation
    — as light-years ago a star
    was born, yet only now is seen
in that first/final conflagration.

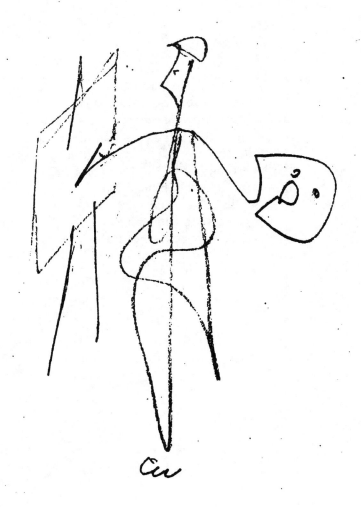

SPIDER

At
the centre
of your dread
design you crouch —
omnivorous sky-fisherman
whose net is blowing everywhere — spun
cables knitting   air to air and
   nothingness   to nothingness —
invisible strong   cables made
of light and thinner than a
glisten — death's dragnet
waiting for some
arrogant winged
tanglefoot
to light

GOLDFISH

                    gold
          fish
in their
     langorous
          long evening
     gowns of gold lamé
shimmer/shimmy
               round a round
                    aquarium, and now
                         they glide up close
                              and pose, and shop
                    us with big
                    googly eyes
               and lavish lips —
          then swish away,
     all twitch and
          coquetry
               and leave no
     glimmer of their glamour,
          no trace of grace
                    except a flaunt of
                         fantail fins,
          an effervescence
                    where
     their langorous
long evening gowns   once   were   o
                                      o oo
                                         oo
                                          8 o
                                             o

SLUG

What.kind.of.life.is.that.
feel.ing.one's.in.fin.it.es.im.al.
slow.way.a.round.the.eye.less.world,
a thoroughly offensive bit of slime,
its whole intelligence a twitchy
pair of paranoid antennae
to fathom Plato, Aristotle, God Himself
(whom some of us have meant to serve
but with, in truth, more trust, humility
than that totally defenceless bit of spit?)

CRICKETS

History is embarrassing.
Baron, knight and king
demanding thanegeld, tithes,
our very whoreson lives
beneath one banner or another

while crickets
deep in the blood-nourished grass,
black-coated choristers who tickled
their Creator's ears with cricketings,
in domains of green leisure, sang.

SHEBA

So here I am,
    a Siamese
on minikin felt feet
patrolling our shared house
to which my sad meows,
my deadpan flower-face
and ginger-ale pale eyes
may lend a cool cachet,
a certain sly panache
as, curled up in my
window seat at noon
I muse, and muse, and muse
on My Most Tender Mouse.

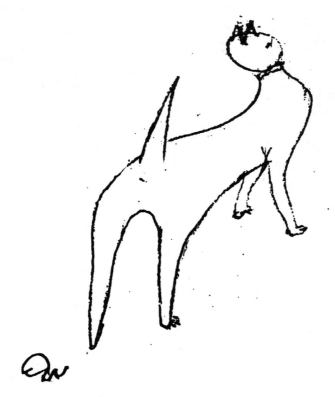

DOGS

Two shaggy hounds,
four footed
footpads,
sniff
each other, pounce:
bounce back
and rock
upright on hind
legs in dancing play,
a wooly wild ballet
of hairy withers, flanks
and snapping fangs
as they fence
and parry
with stiff paws —
dogjuice slobbering
from slubber jaws;
two shaggy friends
leering ear to ear
as they stumble,
tumble over
hurtless in the
happy grass.

SEA LIONS

No more to clap
slap-happy flippers
for a crowd's applause,
no beachballs on noses,
no bobbing and weaving
their keeper to please
with his kettle of kippers
— escaped from some circus,
they fish in the Fraser
poking bare faces
blacker than licorice,
slicker than grease,
above the frolicking waves,
the salmon-filled river.

SEASCAPE

The basso profundo of the sea.

A progenitive blue thunder
cracks
the seawall, smacks
the sperm-soaked crevices in rocks.

A child builds castles out of sand,
sand the colour of moondust,
the colour of those to whom
hello, good-bye have no meaning.

Strobed by the sun, the seafoam
sizzles out along the shore
where freeform algae flagellate,
and screaming gulls whitewing away . . .

the fatuous falsetto of their cries:

the basso profundo of the sea.

SEABUS

One of those
blue blowzy days,
sunglint rocketing
off rocks as our
SeaBus backs
out into the bay.
Hackles of
white chop.
Sprees of spray.
Gullwings furling
and unfurling
in our wake . . .
til North Vancouver
comes in view:

20 storey high
steel pterodactyl
cranes as delicate
as dragonflies
hovering onshore
as swift snowfields
ski toward us as we dock
— one lone loon bobbing
in our aftershock,
one happy flag
having an orgasm
with the wind, and
not one cloud
in the sky.

REGATTA

A
clean
white
isosceles
of sail, wave
cleaving hulls
unrolling somersaults
of foam around the prow
as white seagulls' oscillating
wings battle the black air above
the bowsprit plunging through
sou'wester gales half swallow in
their swells rope-tangled decks awash
and sloping to sea-fingers catching at
the crew leaning backward over nowhere
from slant gunnels,
balancing their lives
against the waves.

SAILOR SONG

Where the horizon ends

out in the centre of the homeless sea
where shadows wave like grass
on the somnambular cold
lip gloss of the waves

Farewell to the fair
weather girls
the drowned sailors sing
as they lie in the mermaid arms of the sea,
lifting and falling, caressed
by green fingers

in the arms of the mermaid sea
until their shoulders turn to foam,
their arms and legs to shoreless foam
in the arms of the siren sea

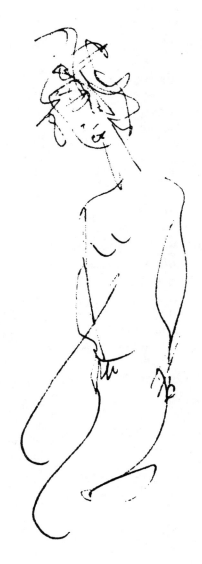

DOING TIME

As some are sent to prison
to gain release from time
and learn inner peace,

at the end of things,
the apple eaten
and the core,
we'll know our crime:
how Adam woke from a deep sleep
to find the woman of his dreams
locked in his arms

and both stood up
innocent, without a leaf
between them and strolled
the primordial first forest
in their primrose prime

before the serpent fell
coil by winking coil
out of the delicious tree
to spoil it all —

for them, and you and me
who languish in the jail
of time although the bail
is paid in full by persons
in high places.

39

CHRISTMAS EVE

Down
at the wounded
doorway of the soul
where all men jackknife, break,
and are remade with pleasure
in Time's cave
(machined by Eve
rotating with clasped Mars),
bent-kneed through straw,
his hands like stars,
the wordless, wet
incarnate Word
appears.

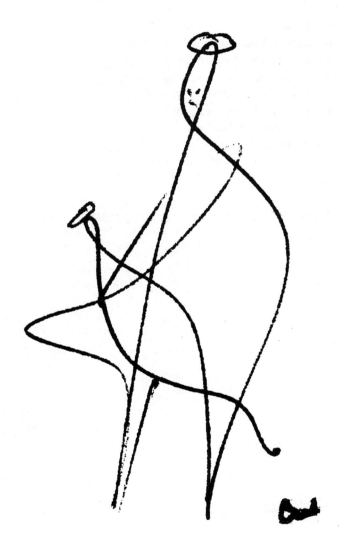

CHRISTMAS LIGHTS

Let there be light —
kilowatts of carols in the night,
tulip-coloured voices singing praise
and choruscating through the highrise skies —
each balcony a blaze of jazz, of jubilate light,
blue/green/blue/green/blue/green jellybeans of light
blinking with the light we have within (O spark
of faith more than a blitz of glitz!) the very light
of very Light reflected in the hollyberry eyes
of children slogging home with sleighs
who see a rainbow through the dark
and turn toward the light.

SLEDDING

Snow has left
      the hills, no
trace of sleighs now, no
sound of hissing runners, cry
      of kids, who bellyflop and float
          — eyes shut against the sleet,
bones shuddering against the varnished slats
      as they bomb the bumps and fly
          out of body, steer
              face frozen into space
                  sleighs almost jumping
                      from sweat-mittened hands
before they bang back to whizzing ice,
      chuting through the alabaster hills,
          down twisting breathless catastrophic slopes
              (the heart-of-darkness moon above,
                  the cold a second skin upon their skin)
                      and snow-stars all around them on the ice
                      cold longest evening of the year.

CHAPEL

✝

UP
LIFTED
HANDS
RAISE
STEEPLES
BUILT FROM
BREAD AND PRAYER,
TWIN BELFRIES
WHERE OUR SOULS ARISE
DISCARNATE TO THE ONE
WHO WAITS IN PARADISE
BESIDE AN ANCIENT THRONE.
BUTTRESSED WITH LIVING BONE

OUR STAINED WINDOW EYES
REFLECT THE SUN ABOVE —
THE HEALED AND HOLY ONE
WITHIN HIS CHAPEL THERE

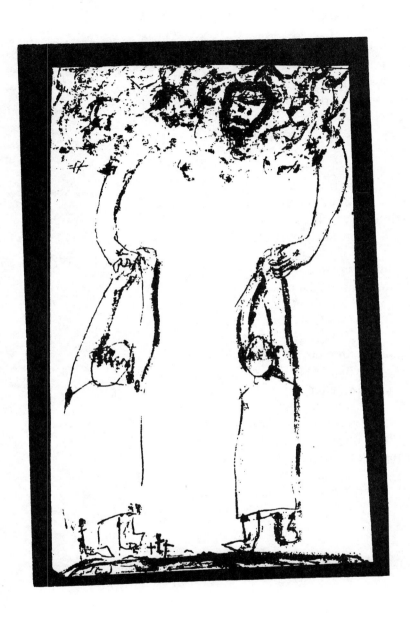

DIVISION

Deep
    in the dark
        obstetric sea
we first learned division,
        how to multiply,
            bearing remnants
of the zygote's parturition
    in twin arms and legs
        and the Great Divide
itself from which you and I
    were lately hurled
        from paradise —
but not before we swam
about as chromosomes,
    part of the First Cell,
      the splitting image
        of the great I AM,
weaned from innocence into the
apple mischief of the world
    by slow increments of eons, ions,
      — the first pseudopod
        reaching its tumescent mass,
breaching its eurythmic wall
becoming two-four-eight and then
      innumerable small
    ad infinitum scions.

Until the double helix, egg,
      mother fish, maternal ape
and lastly, the first human
         learning how to think,
to word his wonder, climb
      beyond the peccadilloes
of loaned flesh, beyond
the frugal landscapes of this world,
      beyond the grim grave-grasp of time
         to Him who, neither That nor This,
            is Both and More — and
            without division.

LUST AND ENVY

As the ghost of a poem
    is more impressive
than the words that betray it,
    our thoughts change matter
      as an axe chops wood.

As horseflies cruise
    the stench of garbage,
    Lust and Envy
with their screaming eyes
    and flaming hair, breed hate
      in those whose appetites
        nothing can assauge

— while those who feed
    lost animals are fed
      by their own kindness
        as an inner light
      guides those who turn
a blind eye to tv.

Lust
and Envy

THE PARACLETE

Brother of the poor,
the soul's most welcome guest
(bringing your own dinner)
best friend
and wise consoler,
source of life and love,
more swift than any motion,
creator of the world — the Breath
which Earth and sea exhaled and
all creatures from Leviathan to ant
— time's executive assistant
at our birth and at our death,
companion of both saint and sinner,
eternal light, all-seeing Dove —
within to give us strength,
in front to guide...above
to grant us blessings at the end.

THE NATURAL GALLERY OF ART

— for Susan McMaster
and Stephanie Bolster

The zebra bark of birch,
catkins hanging from the willow,
the casual perfection of a field of hay

are more impressive than a Rubens,
more harmonious than a David Milne,
leaving nothing to delete or add.

Nature knows where the best paintings are.
Corots in the poplars freckling with leaves
the still, misty morning air,

Soutines in a splash of slashing green,
Tom Thomsons in the melancholy mauve
of an alder grove at evening;

intrinsic in each blade of grass
precision greater than an Ingres or Dégas.

ROCK GARDEN

Lobelias and lilacs,
    baby's-breath, nasturiums,
        give this concrete cul-de-sac
an air of rural innocence,
    a pastoral perfume,
      the delicate cool colours
of marimba music on an ocean cruise,
    at the end of a long day that
        led me down the garden path
           not to heartsease, tulips,
but to exhaustion, noise.

And so I thank
    all those who spend some time
        on their knees as if in prayer,
getting down and dirty with their plants;
    working with green thumbs and patience,
garden hose and compost, secret Powers,
    pollen, bees in every kind of weather —
    drunk on daisies — growing-things
      whose very names are flowers:
        sweet alyssum, love-lies-bleeding,
        kiss-me-quick.

TREES

Every tree
has its silhouette:
maple crown, cone
of conifer, tall
column
of the tamarack.
Stretching from each trunk,
concentric limb on limb
fan out in planispheres
of foliage between
the brown utilitarian
hard earth and
the soft green
promissory sky
where clouds and leaves,
sponging up the sun,
overlap the azure edge
of time-eternity;
and wave their hands
in a shadow-dance
of cloudy leaf
and leafy cloud
in greenwood atrium,
cherry
orchard,
city
slum:

most grow
in crowds, a few
stand alone
on the farthest hills
wearing heaven like a halo,
yet each one has its story:
their jillion leaves
rehearse the lives,
the loves,
the untold history
of lost neighbourhoods.
Those who died or moved away
still live invisibly
in boughs that breathe
their whispered names
no longer mute
but rising from root-
nourished memories,
leafing out each spring
on spreading branches,
rustling in the breeze,
giving dust a voice
in maple grove,
forest room
or city
slum.

PART SONG

Swanwhite
the mountain
as snow-white the swan:
and as the lake is blue
lakeblue the sky.

Grassgreen
the grass snake
as snakegreen the grass;
and as blood red the rose
rose-red the heart

— so all things
interweave, imply
all varied Nature one,
each sunning marigold
a marigold gold sun.

ICARUS

As feathered Icarus once crashed
into the sun and was ecstatically
consumed by flame,
we fly toward our immolation,
each day a wingclap closer
to no everlasting night
but to a place of pure elation
where, unselved, dissolved into pure light
our headlong, torched, incinerated frame
will bear the Son's consummate shame,
and share in his perfection at the last.

ICARUS I - ASCENSION

ICARUS II — ECSTACY

ICARUS III – IMMOLATION.

THE JOURNEY

No one can decode the future,
the long voyage to cancer,
the soul germ-free at last.

No less surely than the lamb
or as cliffs of cloud wave-polished
by the sea and soon demolished
by the shadow of a wind,
the virgin and the unicorn will die.

Nothing is spared because of its beauty.

As darkness, reddened by the sun,
takes on the patina of morning,
we move toward wisdom,
a place beyond pleasure, pain,
each day a reassessment of the past.

QUIXOTE ∞

FATHERS

Let us praise those who at dawn
slip from comfortable beds
armed for work, the Forty Years' War
with frustration, fatigue,
turning time into bread,
giving their strength to us
still asleep in warm blankets.

Let us praise those who grow old
devoted to daughters, sons;
forgiveness their gift,
humour their craft,
their skill an amazing patience,
enjoying as theirs our success,
by example teaching us wisdom.

Intensive Care Unit

Eyes glazed
with too much looking
at the unseen,

he has no words now;
only touch;
laying my hands within
my father's thin
cold hands

here in his last room
making his last
stand,

we are one —
as he is one
with the sparrow
on his window ledge
poised for take-off

into another air

LABOUR

Who built the pyramids?
Who built the C.P.R.?
Not Cheops,
not Van Horne
with his own railway car,
but countless myriads
of the living dead
for whom morning
had no meaning
except soul
destroying toil.

Everything that's built
was made by hands, the back
breaking labour, aching
muscles, bones
of the Nameless Ones
exploited, crushed,
down through the
timeclock ages,
remembered on the pages
of no history; honoured
by no statue, plaque

— those more anonymous
than the stones
they lifted
and at last became:
the Faceless Ones
ground down to raise
another's fortune, fame,
for whom morning
had no meaning
except work, or worse:
*un*employment, shame.

ENTREPRENEUR

— Bob Webster

Pushing a swollen shopping cart
overflowing with failure
stacked in garbage bags,
he trudged the back lanes
of his mind, on lookout for
discarded cardboard, bottles, cans,
anything to trade for a few coins.

Crouched in some alley alcove,
whacked out on smack or booze,
without the hope of hope,
the consolation of despair,
lost in a labyrinth of voices
shouting die, he lay down one night,
pulled the snow around him, froze.

CHINATOWN

By the doors of honeysuckle houses
little mirrors to waylay the dead.

On a window ledge
a doll-like Buddha smiles
across continents and eons
at Chevy trucks that line the curb.

The smell of firecrackers, joss.

Behind a courtyard wall
ceramic lions and dragons pounce
where old men, fragile as their
shadows, play at draughts

and dream perhaps of cherry trees
hung with paper lanterns
in a heaven of young maidens
bringing tea and singing Cantonese
in high sweet singsong voices.

FLY AT MY WINDOWPANE

He does not know
his days, as yours and mine,
are in another's hand
nor does he comprehend
how he is watched —
as we are watched.

With that subtle, sly
clairvoyant smile
my mother had,
I look at a trapped fly
batting his life out
at the buzzing glass —

so near and yet so far
from where he wants to be,
as I am from that sky
calling me by name
through the windowpane
of time, into eternity.

NEW YEAR'S EVE

silence

the silence
of incense

        burning

            and then

      an ebullient
      abandon

of bells

        while the new year
        yawns in his crib

and the old one

         wanders

            away

      and the dancers sway
        like paper streamers
            as the floorshow starts
          amid the screams and
      shouts of laughter

in the whirling
    ballroom of the

         whirling

      world

ENVOI

Ideal and Real are one
as the earth prepares our food
from horse manure, seed and sun;
as invisible atoms form all things,
whirling through duckweed and the duck,
the welder and his torch,
the blue dome of a church
and the parishioners within.
We live in vast cathedrals of the soul
and yet see nothing but a narrow cell.

Woman is the image of man's love
as Nature is the source of art,
as flute and twelve-stringed cithera
are the sound of those upwinged
on invisible swift currents to the sky
where everything's preserved forever,
the fire in the cinder long burned out,
the flight of birds long turned to dust.

For those who were born
to be neither fathers nor mothers,
but the parents of poems, I write;
but whether I write or not
the poems will always be there
neither marvelous nor strange
but as common as pebbles
waiting for someone to gather,
take home and cherish as children.

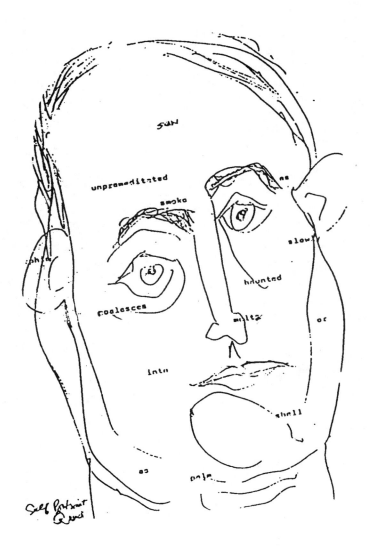